THE HARD WORD BOX

Sarah Hesketh is a poet and freelance project manager. She holds an MA in Creative Writing from UEA and her work has appeared in a number of magazines and anthologies including *The White Review, Soundings, Catechism: Poems for Pussy Riot* and *Binders Full of Women*. In 2007 her collaboration with composer Alastair Caplin was performed at the Leeds Lieder Festival. Her first collection of poetry, *Napoleon's Travelling Bookshelf,* was published by Penned in the Margins in 2009. In 2013-14 she was a poet in residence with Age Concern Central Lancashire.

ALSO BY SARAH HESKETH

Napoleon's Travelling Bookshelf (Penned in the Margins, 2009)

The Hard Word Box

Sarah Hesketh

Penned in the Margins

LONDON

PUBLISHED BY PENNED IN THE MARGINS
Toynbee Studios, 28 Commercial Street, London E1 6AB
www.pennedinthemargins.co.uk

The right of Sarah Hesketh to be identified as the author of this work has been asserted by her in accordance with Section 77 of the Copyright, Designs and Patent Act 1988.

First published 2014

Second edition published 2016

Printed in the United Kingdom by Lightning Source

ISBN
978-1-908058-22-5

CONTENTS

INTRODUCTION   7

ACKNOWLEDGEMENTS   11

Service User Belongings on Admission   19

Spoons   20

Into the White   21

Spices   22

Peggy   23

How to Tell It   24

Music for the Brain   25

Make-up   26

George   27

Someone Else's Slippers   38

Trudie   39

Phyllis' Instructions for Sex   40

Ron   41

Marlene   43

Doreen   58

Partially Fixed Strings   59

Left Brain   60

Hide and Seek   61

All the Reasons Why Mollie Can't Go Home   62

Right Brain   64

Interview with the Bears   65

Elizabeth   66

Angela   72

The Hard Words   82

Communion   83

Jack   84

This Place   87

INTRODUCTION

"When you tell this story, make sure you tell it right."

It was my last day at Lady Elsie Finney House, and I was saying goodbye to some of the residents and K, a member of the care staff. Although initially confused about what a poet might be doing in a dementia care home, K had warmed to me over the nine months of my residency. She saw the value in trying to get the attention of the outside world on issues surrounding dementia. She had spoken honestly with me about how she wished she had more time to spend just chatting or doing activities with the people in her care, and she had made it clear how undervalued she felt – both by her own managers in the care sector, and by society as a whole. "Just remember us, and tell it right," she said, and then went on dispensing medication, shunting her trolley around the day room. I nodded and smiled, the same way I had seen residents nod and smile, when they were told that it wasn't time for lunch yet or that they couldn't go home today: I had absolutely no idea how I could ever respond to her request.

For 20 weeks in 2013, I took an early train out of Euston each Friday morning, and spent the day at Lady Elsie Finney House in Preston. Lady Elsie Finney House is a secure residential care home, designed for people with dementia. It's modelled on a New England clapboard farmhouse and there are three 'wings' — Willow, Saffron and Amber — each of which houses up to 15 people at a time. Each resident has their own room, plus access to a day room and bathrooms. Many of the residents are immobile and require moving in a hoist. Almost all require help going to the toilet or washing; a small number no longer speak, or communicate only through facial expressions, physical movements and/or other noises.

I was there as part of an artist-in-residence programme with Age Concern Central Lancashire. Funded by Arts Council England, *Where the Hearts Is* was the first project of its kind in the UK: an artist-in-residence scheme that aimed to go beyond the usual approaches of art therapy. We were not there to help residents produce watercolours or embroider cushions. The project posed the question: what would happen if you placed practising contemporary artists in dementia care settings and asked them to create responses? We were encouraged to collaborate positively with the people we met, but not to make comfortable art. If we uncovered some difficult truths along the way, that would be ok. In the care sector, art is often used as a PR tool, or a way of putting a positive gloss on some dark situations. Age Concern and the project management team wanted us to "tell it right" as well, but what "right" might mean in these circumstances was largely up to us to discover.

To begin with, I felt at a real disadvantage compared to some of my fellow artists. Dance or painting — these were activities that already happened regularly in the centres we were visiting. People were comfortable with the idea of them, and they seemed to offer more obvious ways to get to know people. Poetry isn't the most popular topic at the best of times, and for the residents I was working with, language was something difficult; something they now had to fight with; something, even, to be afraid of.

What I hadn't anticipated was how quickly, when people are no longer trusted to speak for themselves, language and texts begin to accrue around them. One of the first things I had to do was learn the language of care: people are 'service users'; looking after people is 'person-centred care'; you don't suffer from dementia, you are a person with dementia. Then I became fascinated with the language of the care plans that are produced for each resident. These plans are meant to provide a record of a person's interests, their likes and dislikes, so that staff can develop a better understanding of the people in their care. The result was a strange set of profiles comprised of often random-seeming details. Just as people begin to struggle to articulate clearly who they are, a whole set of alternative identities are being created for them.

A number of poems in this book combine real phrases from these care plans with the actual words that people said to me. Some of these poems are found poems, taken from posters and instructions around the home. The poem 'Elizabeth' is made up of every word that Elizabeth said to me during my 20 visits. The three longer pieces are edited transcripts of interviews, and I'm incredibly grateful to George, Marlene and Angela for taking the time to tell me their stories.

When I first started working on *Where the Heart Is* I thought my job would be like that of an archaeologist. That I would help people to recover who they had been, and explore new ways to hang on to that. Instead, I realised what was most important, was not that Maureen used to like jazz, or that Bill had once been a butcher, but that Jack tells great jokes, Phyllis likes helping others to the table — that's who these people are now. They are still living their lives, and these lives are what need to be represented — in art, in policy, to families. Especially if the lives people are living in care are to change for the better.

A number of the residents died during the time I was visiting

Lady Elsie Finney House, including Ron, Angela and Elizabeth. It was a real privilege to spend time with people and their families at this point in their lives.

If the experience of reading this book is a little disorientating, then that is probably a good thing. If I learnt anything at all, it's that the experience of dementia is different for absolutely everybody; 'telling it right' would have been an impossible, and in some sense, pointless task. Here are some of the people I met. Here are some of the things we said. Sometimes there isn't anything else.

Sarah Hesketh

Discover more about the project at wheretheheartispreston.tumblr.com

ACKNOWLEDGEMENTS

I would like to thank the editors of the following publications in which some of these poems, some in altered versions, have appeared: *DIAMetric* and *Writing in Education* (NAWE).

I would like to thank Age Concern Central Lancashire, especially Judith Culshaw, Alex Walker and Kath Wilkinson, for the fantastic opportunity to work with them as an artist in residence. It was an incredible experience and I'd like to thank all the staff, residents and relatives at Lady Elsie Finney House in Preston who took the time to share their stories with me. My special thanks to Marlene Kendal, whose honesty and enthusiasm for raising awareness about dementia and its impacts was an inspiration.

My thanks also to my fellow artists in residence on the *Where the Heart Is* project: Chiara Ambrosio, Sarah Butler, Jennifer Essex and Liam Walker.

Special thanks and love to my family for their support, Hannah August for her editorial notes, David Clegg, without whom nothing would ever happen, Tom Chivers for his eternal patience, and Padraig Reidy for all the love and all the chicken.

For the residents of Lady Elsie Finney House, past and present.
And for my grandma, who never has two eggs.

'... always the hard word box they wanted'

Mimnermos: The Brainsex Paintings, Anne Carson

THE
Hard Word Box

Service User Belongings on Admission

White knickers   10 pairs   (named)
Silk   full body underskirt   (named)
Floral dressing gown   pink and black   (unnamed)
Cardigans   x2   pale blue (unnamed)

Handbag   one dark   large in size   flowered pattern
Hair brush   x1   lilac handle   smiley face

Toilet bag   x1   lilac see-through   contains:
Toothbrush and case   x1   clear plastic
Toothpaste   x1   small tube   fresh mint
Soap in clear case   x1   Plus comb

Handkerchiefs   x3   white   (unnamed)
Dresses   x2   blue patterned   (unnamed)
2 x flannel   one pink   one blue

Tights   x5 pairs   nude
Shoes   x1 pair   black

Kit Kat   x3   packs and bars
Television chair   x1   brown

Suitcase   x1   small   red

Pictures   x4:   2 cream frames
          1 silver   1 black

Spoons

Spoons break up the day.
Yes. No. Out of mouths
  wedged in the spaces
between who and when. In
  bookshelves and along
windowsills, bright slugs
  who came in for the night.
Such shiny visitors,
  they give us back to ourselves,
our faces strangely curved.
  Small windows into tiny worlds
we hold to impossible angles.

Into the White

They say the colour of finally is
red.   The dinner plates, the walls, the chairs
are all saying: look! you live by emergency.

Everything is so
balled heart. Too much muscle
   in the sound of thinking.

All we want is to be allowed
to be gone.
                        To fall from this dark like

      brushed white chalk.

Spices

The following SPICES principles apply:

Social : Outings, conversation, hair care, hobbies and activities.

Physical : Bathing, toileting, nutritional needs, laundry, hair care.

Intellectual : Reading (books, magazines available).

Cultural : Acceptance, diet, dress values.

Emotional : Support, touch, talking, listening.

Spiritual : Visits to church, mosque or temple. Visits by clerics, rabbis. Allowing discussions re religion/death/life etc.

Peggy

My name is Margaret, but I prefer to be called Peggy.

I have lots of memories that make me smile, but I can't choose a favourite one at this moment.

I feel happy when I am surrounded by my family.

I enjoy going to my son Graham's house and sitting in his garden under the big tree.

I don't like being on my own as I like a lot of company.

I feel upset when my family has visited and left to return.

I like to put my make-up on every day and have my hair done at the hairdresser's weekly.

I am a Roman Catholic but I do not attend church at present, which is my own choice.

I am not one for hobbies as such.

My greatest achievement in life was meeting my husband Walter.

Also meeting Sir Stafford Cripps when I worked at Dan Kerr's.

I consider myself a very independent lady.

I like listening to all kinds of music but mostly I enjoy Country and Western.

I enjoy tidying around, putting things in cupboards.

How to Tell It

Lily seems to have forgotten that she has previously told the story. But what is striking is that when she retells it, she does so in almost identical words. She may have forgotten telling it but she has not forgotten how she told it.

A beginning, a middle and an end.
This much she remembers:
you must never begin your story with the weather.
It is important to have rounded characters, but you
should resist the chocolate taste of cliché.
Adverbs are terrorists; murder your darlings.
If a gun appears in the second act, well,
try your very best not to lose it.
Ideas should walk into a room without arriving.
The very best narrators tell lies.
Show don't tell, but a tale never loses
in the slow breath of its telling.
This much she remembers:
a beginning, a middle, an inhalation.

Music for the Brain

CLAP CLAP CLAP
why are we? CLAP
CLAP *COME ON!*
PACK UP YOUR TROUBLES
IN YOUR

mum hated that one
the rude brush it pulled it
howled through my hair
thank God your dad
was a protected trade CLAP

now the jive, she'd say
that's a small person's dance
his hands CLAP *and*
CLAP *my hands*
the whole bruising
heartstart of it

Make-up

What terrible crayons, he thinks,
plucking the pencils from their bag each morning.
He settles her face before him like a mirror,
wondering how to draw her back to him today.
Such greasy bullets of colour; he should be painting
a battle scene or the thick, waxed interior of a heart,
not tricking the memory of blood into her lips,
pinching his own budded mouth to couple hers.
As if these pinks could kiss them back to life.
As if somehow it were possible to be
        still loving and ordinary.

George

George: What's that?

Sarah: That's my pen.

George: [*handles it*] Age Concern? My god, they're thinking about us already. They've got pens out for us at Age Concern! We can still remember you know. You've got nice hands anyway.

Sarah: Oh, thank you.

George: And you've got a ring on. Are you married?!

Sarah: No.

George: Oh, I'm glad you're not. You're in my good books then. I wish I was 21. We'd have a lot more fun then.

Sarah: Would you take me dancing?

George: Nah, I'm not a dancer. That's something I've never... I've always been a footballer. I've never been still with my feet. But I've never ever liked dancing. I couldn't see nowt in it. You're wasting your time. There was a lot of fellas in my younger day used to go dancing.

Sarah: How did you find a wife then, if you didn't go dancing?

George: I dunno. I can't remember how I come to get married. I can't remember that. That's something I can't remember, how I come to meet her... I think everybody liked me. I've never been one for causing trouble. Fighting? Have I heck. That was my favourite thing to say. "You two, bloody grow up!" "Will you never grow up?" "What you doing it for? You'll hit him, he'll hit you. Who's won?!"

That's something... I've not been frightened about, but I just haven't done it. It's never been in me at all. Sport – run or play football and cricket. I've done all that. I've done everything in sport. And even though I say it myself I were pretty good at it. I weren't a dumbo. I weren't just somebody who walked down with a cricket bat and got out straight off, you know. Whatever I tried to do, I tried to make it so... people would say, "Well, he's not a bad player anyway." And snooker, well I learnt, I played snooker when I were about ten. That's when I started.

Sarah: Did you ever make any money at it?

George: Well, bits of money. You never bothered about money in them days. You'd win a few... but it just vanishes, it evaporates. But I learnt in Billy Dole. A relation, one of my relations, he were what you call a manager of the billiard hall. But I were still at school. That was when I started playing snooker. And even though I'm saying it now... they're not here... but at one time I could have beat anybody. But I made it my business to beat them. I didn't just play for a bit of fun and a laugh. I'd concentrate on things. And I'm still not a bad player now, though I don't do much playing. But I can do it, just the same. Never leaves me. The only thing, I've not been a fighter. I've never fancied it. It's not that I can't do it. I probably could do it. But

I used to say what do you wanna fight for? You hit me and I hit you. Who's best off then? Because if we do, I promise you, whatever we do, I'll hit you bloody harder than you hit me. No. I've never been a girl man.

Sarah: Now, I don't believe that.

George: No, no. Not really. I like girls. I like them. But they are... the longer I live, the longer they make me happy. George! It's no good saying, "what have I missed?" I could still get it now even though it's older! Ha. I'm sorry.

Sarah: You're all right, George.

George: Better to cry – no, better to laugh than to cry, whatever you do. But it's funny that. When I were younger, I were never a girly man. There were lads liked girls at school and all that but I used to say, I'd rather play football or summat. I've probably been wrong but you don't know. You can't be right all the time. The only thing, I've never been a fighting man. That's something I've often said to myself. I should have been a bloody fighter. I weren't frightened of fighting but I just used to say, grow up. That's one of my favourite sayings, whenever there were any trouble coming. Just grow up. Why don't you two bloody grow up. You know, that were my favourite saying, and it's stuck with me.

The only thing that beats me is my ears. They beat me. I missed things many a time. You've said something there and I don't know what you've said. That happens all the time and it really annoys me. I miss all sorts of things with that. And I don't like repeating myself, saying "What did you say?" Sad thing. But that's a thing that has beat me. And when I think over the years, I can't even think where anybody's tried to do owt about it?

Sarah: Do your hearing aids not work so well?

George: No, well, they've been messing about with them this morning. I can't hear a bloody thing. I don't know what I have these on for. I've had them on a bit now anyway. There's all sorts in today's world. Probably things are a lot better, I don't know. I should have tried some, somewhere, but I haven't done. That's the only good thing about me. I've worked for all kinds of different people. Rich people – in the racing game. But I've never ever touched anything. Never touched money. Mind you, when we're talking about carrying. I've been carrying sometimes for people between five and ten thousand pound. And I've been in charge of telling them what to do, which is a big temptation. And especially when you haven't got so much in your pocket, you know. And they'd probably never find it. Never even think about it. But I've never been a thief. So that's something that's stuck with me. Touch wood. That's a good thing about me, what I've done. But I've had opportunity. If I'd have been a villain, I could have took what I wanted. And I could probably have not got caught. Because when they know you... they assume you won't. When you know who's who and what's what. Once you do something wrong you're out. That's it. You never never in your life get back. Oh, if you ever do summat wrong and you know you've done it wrong, you'd wish you'd never done it. Too late wishing I'd never done it because they know what it is. You're only too aware.

Sarah: Were they good men to work for?

George: That's what's beating me now, talking. I miss things.

Sarah: Were they good men, your bosses?

George: Oh, top men were always top, dead straight men. From what we saw. But behind the tapes, what goes on. You know what I mean? People do all sorts of things in this world. It's a rum world, I tell you. You wouldn't believe it if you put it all down in writing in a book. Somebody would say, that's a load of old cobblers that.

Sarah: You should write that book.

George: Nah. I could roll out some nice tales. I've never done... I can honestly say that I have never, ever in my life, put my hand in the till and took money. I've had all kinds of money on me. When I've been away racing somewhere and we've been winning. Go on George, stick that in your pocket. I've had bloody money all over me. And nobody bothered. They might say how much is there? See – there's a monkey there. Five hundred pound. Or you might have two thousand, three thousand pound if you're winning. But they don't check it. They don't count it for a fiddle. And, touch wood, I've never done it.

Sarah: They say money's not everything.

George: No, but when you've real money. It's a difficult position. Scratting about if you've not got much in your pocket and you've just had... and we hadn't been married long, about that time. But it's never... I've never even thought about pinching money, never. I've had loads of cards and I've never once in life. And he wouldn't have missed it anyway. They probably wouldn't have done but I've never done it. Because once you've done it, oh you do it again. You do it once and get it, guaranteed you'll do it again. The other thing I've not been – I've never been a fighter. I've never been one for fighting. I did try it. I've had a go when I were younger. Doing a bit of boxing, you know. I used to think to myself, what's this nonsense. I never enjoyed it. No, not massively. You hitting me and me hitting you. If it were snooker or owt like that, I'd play anybody. "This kid'll play you!" When I were young, they used to say. "This kid'll play!" And they used to look at me and think... but they always finished up at paying table. I always sent them to pay, you know.

Sarah: Did you bet yourself?

George: What's beating me now is when somebody says something.

Sarah: Did you bet a lot yourself?

George: No, not really. I've not been a gambling man. I might, I dunno. When you're talking about seven days a week. There's all sorts can happen. Once you're amongst gamblers... there are some really thick men. Makes you wonder... I used to sit down at night many a time and think, how the bloody hell did you ever get any money? But somewhere along the line they'd got a business going or some villainy. You know what I mean? That's how people get money. You don't get money with working. Whatever you do, you live to be a hundred years of age! You'll never get rich working. I promise you, not working for somebody. Not unless there's a fiddle somewhere. Oh, I could tell some stories if I could get someone to write the books for me. Some nice tricks and things. But I've never been. I've never stolen any money. Because in them days you know, there's more to come. There was always something happening. Once you do something wrong you'll never get back. They just ignore you. And you don't want that.

Sarah: Is it a business that needs trust?

George: I could have done all sorts of things when I think back. I could write a book, well, I could have done. "And what did you do?" And I'd put: Nothing. "What did you do?" Nothing. And they'd put at the bottom, "Well you must be a mental case, not to do it." And if they never get made... gamblers, they're a different world to us. They're in a different world. And once you're out, you're never, ever back in. But yet they're as good as gold. If you're ill or something, or the family's in trouble, something like that. If you're snowed under – "What do you want?" "What do you need?" It's there. There's good and bad of everybody. What I know of it, anyway. There's bound to be some villains.

Sarah: Did you always work for the bookies?

George: I started out as an apprentice boot and shoe repairer. Up in Lancaster Road. An apprentice boot and shoe maker, that's how I started my life. But I got into racing. When I were young – I were 'appen, fifteen or sixteen, when I started looking at horses and racing and that. I don't think it's the same today as it was then. There was always something happening. But because I've lost it all... I don't know who's the villains and who's not the villains. They might all look the nicest men in the world but they'd shoot you soon as look at you. Somewhere, there'd be somebody like that. But I've never been a fighting man. I'm not saying I couldn't handle myself. But that's something... I've never done it.

Sarah: Were there a lot of people carried guns?

George: Well, you carried a gun and thinking. I don't think I've shot at anybody to say I've shot him. Although there's one or two you might think - I wish I'd have fucking shot him. And I've sworn again there, you see. I'm sorry.

Sarah: That's all right. So you had a gun then?

George: Well, I had a gun but it was always hidden away, so ninety percent of them didn't know I had a gun. I weren't one of them cowboys that used to walk round with my gun in my holster. I didn't like being a cowboy. I'd rather have been a villain.

Sarah: Did you ever use it?

George: Nah, I don't think I ever shot at anyone. I don't think I ever shot at anyone to kill them. I probably shot to frighten them off. I dunno... when I think of myself then. What you see is what I am. I just don't bother. I've probably missed all sorts of things in my life. Especially girls. There's all sorts of girls isn't there? Good girls, bad girls, nice girls, naughty girls. But I've not been one, anyway. I've not been one for chasing girls. They don't want me, or they can want me.

Sarah: Well, you did get married.

George: Yes, I did get married. But I can't remember... we are... at least I think we're still together. I'm a bit... upset in my mind at the moment about it. I don't know, somebody's not been so well and I don't know if my wife's all right or not. You know? You know sometimes I go home and sometimes I don't go home and they might not see me for a few months or something like that. I know it's wrong, it's wrong. I should be turning all that in now, at my age. Nonsense.

That's one thing about me. I've laughed. I've had plenty of laughs in my life. I hate being a stubborn and awkward bugger. I'd rather laugh. The only thing that annoys me now is my ears. Because I miss things. Sometime I laugh when I should have cried. But I've never been a fighting man. Not because I'm frightened, I've boxed... when we were about sixteen, but I never liked it. I used to say, we're wasting our bloody time. Boxing! Who invented this little game? Boxing!

Sarah: Where did you play football?

George: I started off at school. I were the captain, captain of the school football team. And I played twice on at Preston North End when I were a schoolboy. We won one and drew one. So I've got medals for them at home. I still have them, I haven't thrown them away. And I've played football for different teams. Big lads team and all that. I weren't a bad player even though I say it myself. If I'd been a lump of wood I wouldn't have done it. Owt where I can't do it, I'd just retire from it. But I've always been... suitable, you might say. But not with the girls, I've not been a girl man so I haven't had time wasted chasing girls. I probably could have had plenty of girls but I've not been a chaser. All I can say is, what you see is what you get. If you like it, you can have it. If you don't like it, you can lump it. But I wouldn't do owt wrong, I wouldn't ever hurt her. I wouldn't ever hit a girl or owt like that. Over sex or that. That's a little lads' game that anyway, isn't it? You either like it or you don't like it. If you like it enjoy it, and if you don't like it well, lump it. And if you don't get married then you get to forty or fifty and think bloody hell, I wish I had. Well, it's too late then, you can't do it. You can't turn that clock back.

The only thing I've wished, really, not really wished... Right through my life from beginning to end... from starting from scratch... when you're scratting about and you have nowt... and then you get struggling for money and summat goes wrong and you can't get this and you haven't got that. Them's the bad times, you know. That's where somebody comes out with, guns coming out. In them days you were talking about... if you wanted money... you just got a gun somewhere off somebody and you'd be bound to get some money. But I've never... I wouldn't do it now. Even if I had nowt. I have nowt at this moment in time. But I've never bothered about money. If anybody wants summat and I have it in my pocket I give it them. That's the end of it. I must be wrong in my mind. I think I've fucking had them and helped them. That's the way it works. But it comes back round. It's like the merry-go-round. One minute you have nowt and then next minute the merry-go-round's come back and you say, oh we're off again! It's a good life, really you know. You might get involved with something boring where you'd be bored to death. But you can't get out of it. You want to do summat else and you can't.

But I can't grumble. I've not been a dumbo at the game. I can pick something up. I can soon tell the wheat from the... what do they call it... from the chaff. But what you see of me really is what I am. I've gone through life as I am. If I'd have been a fighter I'd have been a bad man. If I'd have been a fighter. But I've been in charge of this and... things I shouldn't say... but it died off me. I don't think I could do it now. I've got out of the villain's game. I've given up wanting to be a villain. I don't carry guns anymore. I just plod on.

Someone Else's Slippers

The prince visits every day.
He must, she reasons.

How else to explain her feet
stuffed like potatoes into a cocktail glass?

How else this cuff and its sorry
drip from her hand,

these teeth purring against her gums,
the itch of someone else's kisses?

Even her eyes are not her own;
she wants to tell the woman next to her:

it's ok, I see what it is
you've been trying to tell us all along.

The prince visits every day.

Someone, somewhere in here,
she thinks, must be the real Cinderella.

Trudie

Trudie shows me her breasts
and they are
marsupial, such
nutty brown sacks
their nipples point
groundwards as if to say
let me go, gentleman,
I've put down my guns.
I want to clutch them and
give them back to her,
return these still warm
eggs to the nest.
But they're gone,
narrow secrets
she no longer knows
she keeps;
the small, twin
carcasses of wrens
hung up like winter meat.

Phyllis' Instructions for Sex

All women really need
is a thing they can
pull out sometimes,
and then fold away quietly
when they're done.

Ron

Ron's sister is very important to him.

Ron likes to be dressed smartly at all times, with a hankie in his
pocket.

Ron likes people to talk to him quietly and slowly so he can
understand them.

Ron enjoys both tea and coffee with sugar and has a good appetite.

People must be patient with Ron.

Ron needs the assistance of two members of staff with all his
personal care needs.

Ron went to school in Kendal.

Ron enjoyed football and drawing at school.

Ron had a hard childhood having been brought up in a children's
home from the age of five.

Ron's first paid job was on a farm. He was a farm labourer. He was
also in the army and has been a removal man.

Meeting his sister for the first time was Ron's most special occasion.

Ron enjoys the company of people, especially when having a pint
with them in the pub.

Ron likes to have a routine.

Ron did not go to church and doesn't follow a religion.

Ron still likes to listen to music and being in the garden in nice
weather.

Ron is quite easy going. The only thing that upsets him is if his
routine is broken.

Ron has always been a hard worker and was loved wherever he
went.

Ron had a hard start in life and learnt to stand on his own two feet
very early on.

Ron has a lovely nature and very strong morals.

Ron has always adapted to situations very well.

Ron has always been a quiet person.

Ron would only ever show a different personality if someone upset
him – he would stick up for himself.

All Ron wants for the future is to be comfortable, well fed and
warm.

Ron enjoys listening to music of all kinds, but particularly Roy
Orbison – you can see by his facial expressions and
movements.

Ron has no mobility and requires a hoist for all transfers.

Ron would like to stay as healthy as possible.

Ron tends to express himself by singing loudly towards the end of
the day, and he has a habit of pulling out his tongue.

Ron does not like to see himself in the mirror and can swear and
shout out if this happens.

Ron can show good eye contact when you have a conversation with
him.

Ron has limited sight in one eye. On a day to day basis this does not
really affect him too much.

Ron requires checking throughout the night to ensure he is dry and
comfy.

Marlene

Sarah: When did you first start to notice that Ron was suffering with dementia? Do you think he understood what was happening to him?

Marlene: No, I don't think he did. That's why they get so frustrated in the beginning. Because I think they realise that something's not quite the same. But obviously they don't know what...

Sarah: How old was he?

Marlene: He was just in his late fifties. And he'd been for his couple of pints in the afternoon, so we just thought - oh you know: he's probably had a pint or two, just one more than he should have had.

We just kept noticing, just different little things. Like... they sort of forget that they've eaten. They think they've eaten and they haven't. And then other people started noticing, that he was forgetting a few things. Just stupid little things really. That nobody would think, oh, there must be something wrong with him. He went to stay with a relative and she rang us up. He'd gone out for a pint and she'd given him the key, but by midnight he wasn't back. And he'd forgotten where he was.

So I rang my daughter up and I said, "Will you ring the doctors up and make an appointment?" So she took him and she just said, "Look, some people have shown concern because he's obviously forgetting things." And the doctor said, "Oh well, get him on the table and I'll examine him."

Well... Theresa said he didn't know how to get off the table. He just didn't know how to and... Then of course the doctor did a few more things. And Theresa said, "I think by the time he came out the doctor thought Ron was stark raving mad." They arranged for him to go and see a psychiatrist, and then they did the scans.

Sarah: And did Ron know what he was there for?

Marlene: I don't think he knew exactly. He knew he was having a scan. You could explain things to him. But obviously he got frightened about everything because he... They don't know everything that's happening to them... As long as I was there.

Anyway he had it done. And the next time we went to see the psychiatrist he'd done a diagram for me, and he showed me where the brain cells had died off. And there was more on one side than the other. I think it was more on that left side. Because when I used to sit on the left - this is why I always sit on this side. When I used to sit on the left side he couldn't see me. He was always saying "Where are you?" And I had to say, "I'm here Ron. I'm on this side." And if he slept on the left hand side... he always sleeps on his right... If he got turned over on the left hand side for some reason, he wouldn't straighten up. In the morning, all day, he'd be leaning over to the left side.

Sarah: Was he still in his own home at this point?

Marlene: Yes, he was still in his own home. My daughter used to check in but of course she was working and had two little girls. We put coloured details on his cooker and I used to buy the ready meals, to make sure he got something. I used to buy the ready meals and put big stickers on how long it had to go into the oven, because I didn't dare let him loose with a microwave in case he put tin foil in. With the phone we put everybody's number in and put a big list on the top. He only had to press... I used to ring him every day. But he got he was starting panicking about things. And then one day... there used to be a man who lived two doors up from Ron. One night... luckily, he was in. Ron had gone to his door... and the neighbour said he felt so sorry for him... because Ron had bought these fish and chips home... but he didn't know how to put the key in the door. He said his fish and chips were stone cold. And he said... if he hadn't been at home... It was bitter cold outside.

He was panicking about everything and he wasn't safe. So, I just said, "Well, look, do you want to come and live with us, so that I can keep an eye on you?" And he said yes, yes he would. So that's when he came to live with us. And it's funny how you become a security blanket. Because wherever you go... many a time I turned round and nearly knocked him over... They're just there behind you. Because if you go out of sight, it's "Where are you?" It was just a constant.

And then he started... I mean, he was fine. We used to have some good laughs. I used to take him for a ride in the car and we'd go and have a meal out and come out with the dog. But then he started having these hallucinations. Every time he passed a mirror and he saw himself, he would say, "Who's that bastard there? He's followed us! Why is he following us?" I had to block all the mirrors in his own room. Because they don't recognise themselves.

He started having hallucinations about... I think they go back in time, you see. I think because he was brought up in the home, there was obviously somebody in there that hadn't been very nice to him. And he was having hallucinations about him. And through the night sometimes you'd go in and he'd be shouting and screeching. One night he was nearly ripping the curtains off and he had this chair - he was going to throw this chair at him! And I used to say, "There's nobody there Ron! Ron, calm down!" And he started... he'd have big scratches up his arms. And I'd say, "What have you been doing with that?" And he'd say, "It's him! It's him that's doing it!"

One night I went in and his eyes were all squashed and they looked sore. I said, "What you been doing with your eyes?" And Ron said, "He's nearly tried to poke my eyes out." And he was doing it himself. And he was shifting things around in the room. And Ron would say, "It's him! He's moved them all."

Sarah: Did you have people come to the house to help? Did social services visit?

Marlene: No. The psychiatrist came. He would come once a month to the house to see him. But apart from that, no. No help at all.

The crunch really came when I was at work one day. My husband was downstairs, and he could hear this thumping upstairs. And when he went up to Ron…he found him with a pair of scissors. And he was stabbing the wall because he thought he was stabbing this chap. So he had to go in. I think he'd nearly ripped the wall that night. So we had to section him. That was for about 8 weeks. They put him on this anti-psychotic drug. Once they got him on an even keel he came back home... But then... You have to section them, because they can't give them this drug unless they're sectioned. And what they do is, they start them on a high dose and bring them down to a level where the aggression... because what they were frightened of – I wasn't frightened of him... and I said... when they said to me they wanted my permission to section him... I said, "Oh, no. I want him to come home." And she said, "Well he can't. If he mistakes either you or your husband for this chap you could be hurt." Anyway, they got him on the medication and he came home.

But the first morning after he came home, I went in his room. And he had a carpet in his room. And he'd got out and pooed on the floor.

And I thought, oh no. And I thought well, maybe, maybe it's just a one off. But he did it again the next day. And we had to have the carpet taken up and just have a wooden floor put in. So then I had to get up... I was getting up at four o'clock every morning to take him to the toilet so that he didn't get out. And I was putting in pads and stuff.

I came home one day and I started going up the stairs. And I thought, oh my God - I could smell it. I opened his door and I could see he was in a state. He'd tried to clean it up. And it was everywhere. He was covered in it from head to toe. I couldn't even get into his room without stepping in it. So, what I did...I got towels and put them on the floor from his room to the bathroom. I thought, 'How am I going to get him in the bath?' I got a black bag and I just stripped everything off him and put it in a black bag. I made sure he walked on the towels... Got him cleaned up.

Well, I couldn't even get in his room to get some clean clothes, so I just put this old dressing gown around him and he sat on the stairs. And I had to get buckets of water...Mop myself to his wardrobe...oh it was everywhere...on his bed. It took me two hours. Bucket after bucket. Oh, it was terrible. I had to use loads of disinfectant and open the windows. And I mean... I felt so sorry for him. Because he kept saying, "I'm sorry, I'm sorry." And I said, "No, it's not your fault."

So what I did then, I had to get in touch with the social and I cut my days down to three days and he used to go to daycare. I used to drop him off in the morning when I went to work and pick him up again on the way back. And that worked fine, until his mobility started going. But, what you find... I think from a relatives' point of view. You certainly find out who your friends are. Because we became... luckily, I had an understanding with my husband... because we became very isolated. Because they wouldn't invite you out because... if they did... it's like having a baby. You've got to find a babysitter. So, it becomes too much hassle. And you just don't bother. You've no quality of life.

Well, in the end I had to give up work because of his mobility. I had a wheelchair, but he was anxious all the time, because I was behind him. I was having to wheel him backwards because I was frightened of trapping his legs. And with him being incontinent... you've got bedding every day, you know... you've got a hell of a lot of stuff. And then he'd be yapping until four o'clock in a morning. I was up and down all night.

You'd get him in the shower and he'd decide he'd want to sit down. And I'm thinking well, if you sit down, how am I going to get you out? If you sat him on the toilet, if your back was turned... the next thing he'd be off and it would be all over the bathroom. So you'd to sit there and wait.

I brought him home from his daycare one day and I got him out the car to try and carry him in. But oh, he was screeching his head off. He wouldn't move. He nearly had me on the floor and I had to get hold of his trousers, get him back in the car and I thought, well, what am I going to do? He's screeching his head off. So I thought, right, I'll go in, just lock the car door and let him calm down and then I'll try again. So I come back out. Same thing. Would he? He would not walk, would he heck. And he was hungry, you see. And I wondered if maybe he hadn't had much to eat. So I thought, what I'll do is, I'll make the dinner and I'll feed Ron in the car. If any of the neighbours were looking they probably thought, she's flipped it! But I did. Brought his dinner out. And a pudding. And a drink. And he's sat there, like Lord Muck in the car! So I locked him in. I went in and got sorted out and just kept looking through the window and Ron's just sat there, happy as Larry in the car. When Ted came home I said, "That's it. He can't go to daycare anymore, I can't cope with this." So, I had him at home all the time.

And then one day, I had to go to the doctors. And then they sent me to the hospital, and they said I was going to need a hysterectomy. The doctor at the hospital said, "Look, you're going to have to put your own health first." I knew I was heading for a breakdown. You would get up an odd day to start with and you'd think, I don't think I can cope with this today. But then the next day would be a better day. But it got to the stage where every day I'm thinking, I can't, I can't do this. I can't cope. I didn't. I couldn't be bothered with myself. I didn't want to go out. I was getting to a meltdown.

Sarah: How did your husband feel? He must have been worried about you?

Marlene: Well, he was. But he didn't say anything. And if I used to say to him, "I don't think I can cope with this anymore," he always used to say, "There's only you can make that decision. I can't make it for you." Which now, looking at it, I admire him.

So, I rang the social and said, "Look, I'm going to have to go in for this operation. I need to speak to a social worker." Nobody got back to us. So I rang up again and I said, "I'm waiting for a social worker. I want to know that Ron is settled somewhere for respite. I don't just want to dump him somewhere." I knew I couldn't drive for six weeks after the op. And that's when Ron came here at first.

But the guilt is... I mean... the day I brought him in here... I think because I'd got to the stage where I was near a breakdown... I went home and for about two days I just sat in the house and cried. I felt like a weight had been lifted off my shoulders. But I also felt very very guilty.

Sarah: How long was he at home with you?

Marlene: Seven years. Even after Ron had come here... I think it was fatigue, basically. I was still waking up, thinking... Oh, is that Ron? I could hear him. And then I'm thinking, "Oh no, he's not here." But because I had done it for so long... I could actually hear him. I could hear his voice in the night. And, all I wanted to do was just sit. I didn't want to see anybody. I didn't want to be bothered with anything. I just wanted to sit and just think. As if... If I hadn't had to go in for that operation I suppose I probably would have carried on - until I'd had a breakdown. And after, it was only after, that my husband did say - and the family say... we were really worried about you. But it's funny because... I still haven't forgiven the friends that deserted me. Even now.

Sarah: Do you think they were embarrassed?

Marlene: I don't know. One of them... it was her 60th. And I used to do a bit of catering. And I had Ron. She knew I had Ron. And she said, could I do these chicken drumsticks and quiches for her for this party? So I did that. And then she said, "Would you be able to come and help me?" So, I left Ron with Ted, because he was off that day. I went to her house and helped her... with all her sandwiches and everything. But we couldn't go to the party of course, because we had Ron. My husband took his van and we set it all up and left. And she rang us - I think it was a week later, and she said, "We'd like to take you out for a meal to thank you for doing this work. Would you be able to find somebody to leave Ron with?" And I just said no. No, I wouldn't. And she never said... That was it. We never went out for that meal.

Now if that had been me, I would have said: I'd like to take you out for a meal and you're quite welcome to bring Ron along. Because he still enjoyed going out then. But they didn't want him coming. I would have given them the option. It's like the party, her 60th party... I mean he used to love dancing. Didn't you, Ron? You'd have danced the night away! But... no... And I've never forgotten it.

Sarah: Do you think people are scared?

Marlene: Yes. Because they don't know how. Because obviously their speech goes a bit. But he still understood pretty much everything... I could never have acted like that. And you'll hear the same from everybody. Even people I talk to in here. They all say that. You just lose your friends because they don't want to know. You become a burden, you suppose, because you have a burden. And I think that's why so many carers become isolated. And to me that's a time when you need your friends. Where somebody could go and say, you go up town and do a bit of shopping or, go out and he'll be all right. But they didn't.

Sarah: Has it been useful to talk to other relatives here?

Marlene: Oh yes, it has. You do become a bit of a recluse. My daughter, she'll say to me, "You and dad never go out anywhere now." And of course, Ron still takes up quite a lot of my life. I like to come and see him often. But it's not the same stress. You come in now and you can talk to them and feel that you're doing good and feed him. Whereas at home everything's so frantic. But the guilt is horrendous. It is.

Sarah: And coming to visit - you get to know the other residents as well?

Marlene: Oh yes. And they know you. In fact some of them think you're staff sometimes. They're saying, "Can you make me a brew?" I mean, I don't mind... if you can help the staff. I'll wash up. If they're stuck with something... I don't mind. Because when you've looked after somebody you appreciate that it is very hard work. And a lot of people don't understand. I know what it was like looking after one, but when you've got fifteen? And they're all different characters. You've got to coax people. And what one maybe won't do for one member of staff, somebody else can go five minutes after and they'll do it just like that. I don't think anybody, unless they've looked after somebody or they've worked in this kind of establishment, can know what it's like.

I think the thing that upset me most about Ron was... and I think that was why I did it for as long as I did... because he spent his childhood in a home. And I didn't want him to end his days in a home. Of course everything in the home in them days ran like clockwork. And then the army... You see in those days at fifteen, you had to get out of the home. Everything had to be... and that's I think, what kept him going. We might have noticed probably earlier if it hadn't been for the fact that Ron's life rotated around routine. Because he had that routine he probably carried on longer than he might have been able to.

We used to laugh at him. He'd come and stay with us for the weekend and we'd say stop and have your Sunday lunch before you go back. "Oh no, no. I'm not used to doing that." And I'd say, "Ron, you'd think you were married with six kids, stop and have your dinner." "No, no, I've got to go." And he had a coffee table... because my daughter... he used to laugh at her in the end... He had a little coffee table next to his chair and everything was in regimental order. He'd have his fags there with his lighter; he'd have his change there, all set up. And his ashtray... everything... his pens all in line. And my daughter would go in and say, "I see your table's tidy again there, Ron." But she'd have messed it all about and he'd be saying, "Put that back!" And you'd wait. In about five minutes he'd be there again, sorting it all out. I used to say to her, "You're cruel, you." But then he'd start to laugh because she did it every time.

I think they're very scared at the beginning. Because they follow you round. They know that something's going to happen. And if anybody used to ask... He would get doctors asking him questions and he always used to say to them, "My sister knows what's best."

And everything was, "Ask my sister." "My sister does that and my sister will tell you." They know.

I know once, I don't know what he was doing and, I just said it as a joke, I said, "Oh you daft thing!" And he said, "Don't you call me daft!" He was really very angry. I said, "I'm only joking." And he laughed about it after but, you have to be very careful. It must be horrible to feel that things are slipping away from you and you can't understand why you can't remember anything.

Sarah: It's hard to know now how he would feel and what he would want at this stage?

Marlene: I made a promise to him when he came to live with us. I said, "I'll look after you Ron for as long as I can." And he said, "I know you will, Sis." If his mobility hadn't gone I would still have him. I would probably have carried on.

Sarah: To the detriment of your own health?

Marlene: Oh yes. Well, they told me at the hospital. There comes a time when you've got to think about yourself because, as they said, if you buckle under, what good are you going to be to Ron? And that's what I had to come to. But I think... you do come to it, in the end. I think you do come to a stage where you realise, no, I can't do it anymore. But, it doesn't stop you from feeling guilty. And that's why a lot of relatives carry on. Because it's the guilt. Because you feel like you've let them down.

Sarah: Even if you're doing what's best in a bad situation?

Marlene: People have said to me, "How long can you do it?" Even my husband said to me, he's often said, "How the hell you did that for as long as you did. I'll never know."

And I look now and I think, well, at least now I can come and see him and I'm not rushing about doing this that and the other. One thing that I found was, when you start to become tired and weary yourself, you get very erratic with them. And sometimes I used to have to walk out of his room and think, "If I stay in there I don't know what I'll do." I'd have to come out and count to ten and I'd go in. And I'd snap at him sometimes. And then I'd have to go and give him a hug and say, "I'm sorry, Ron."

You get to the point where that's happening more often. You're getting erratic and then you think, "Well, perhaps now's the time." Because I wouldn't have wanted to carry on until one day I really lost it. Something that I would really regret.

Sarah: You can see how people can get to that position?

Marlene: Oh yes. Definitely. Because it's day and night. I mean, as I say, Ron could still be ranting on at four o'clock in the morning. And then, you'd have to keep going in and checking that he was all right. You never got a full night's sleep.

You know it'll only get worse and worse. He started rolling out of bed so I was forever worried. I bought him a proper cot side to stop him, because I was forever going in and picking him up. And then he was sliding out of his chairs. There's no wonder I got ill because I was doing all that lifting him up. But, I don't regret one minute of it. I'd do it again. I'd definitely do it all over again.

Sarah: And did you look at a few different places when you were looking for a care home?

Marlene: No. I knew this was a good place. The social worker kept trying to ring here and nobody was answering the phone. I was starting to panic because, I was hoping to get him in and settled. And, so, I thought, right. One morning I got him up and dressed, and he'd had his breakfast. And I said, "Just come and have a lie on your bed. Just while I get some jobs done." And I pulled the cot side up and I came up here in the car. Normally, I wouldn't have done that. But I knew he couldn't get out because he didn't know how to get up. He didn't know how to get up and roll over.

So I came up here in the car and she said, "Yes, we've got a space." She said she'd come and assess him. I'm going home with my fingers and my toes crossed and everything, thinking, "Please, let him get in." So I was pleased really when I got him in here. But oh, that day that I brought him. It was horrible. It was one of the worst days of my life. It was as though... he looked so lost. And they tell you not to come in the next day to give them time to settle a bit. Well, I couldn't wait to get in to see him. And he was all right! And I mean as soon... bless him... as soon as he heard my voice!

To Ron: It's because you get your chocolate isn't it?!

That having to let go. I don't regret one little bit of anything that I did.

To Ron: Do we?

Because he's always been a lovely natured person. We used to have some laughs. Even... We used to laugh about the silly things... because he'd have a jumper on - but with a t-shirt on top of it. And he'd come down and I'd just burst out laughing and I'd say to him,

"Are you going out dressed like that?" And he'd just look and... he didn't get upset. He'd just laugh with me and we'd laugh about it and then I'd say, "Oh, you've got yourself a new fashion."

Doreen

Doreen is a widow.
Doreen has one son and a daughter-in-law in the Preston area.
Doreen loves flowers.
Doreen loved   [HORRIBLE HORRIBLE HORRIBLE HORRIBLE]
gardening and was always happy when spending time in the
garden.
Doreen likes   [I DIDN'T COME BACK. YOU CAME BACK]
Collie dogs [YOU AND THAT WOMAN] and looking at pictures of
them.
Doreen can be quite unhappy when assisted with personal care.
Doreen likes going into the garden.
Doreen sometimes likes a   [SHUT UP SHUT UP SHUT UP SHUT
UP]   sing-a-long.
Doreen   [DON'T COME ANY NEARER. YOU'RE PAST IT NOW]
likes her own space and to be left alone sometimes.
Doreen doesn't like to be fussed.
Doreen is not tactile.
Doreen used to make all her own clothes [MUCKY MUCKY
MUCKY MUCKY PEOPLE]   as she was so petite she was never
able to find things to fit.
Doreen has a good sense of humour.
Doreen can be a bit rude sometimes   [BE GOOD BECAUSE WE
HAVE NO MORE]   but staff help her with this.
Doreen's Life Achievement: Awaiting Information.
Doreen does not   [THAT'S HORRIBLE. DISGUSTING. NO, I
DON'T LIKE THAT]   mobilise.

Partially Fixed Strings

In fact, the vast majority of formulaic expressions are not completely fixed, and a more plausible model of how they are processed allows them to be only partly specified, while containing gaps for variable items. It will still be quicker to process a single unit with the option to insert coffee, tea, coke, etc. than to construct the entire sentence from scratch.

Alison Wray, 'Patterns of formulaic language in Alzheimer's disease: implications for quality of life'

I've always been a ____.
Never been a ____.
Never had a ____.

Should have been a ____.
Yes, please, I'd like a ____.
Is this the way to ____?

I need to get to ____.
No, I don't want to ____.
Why is everything ____?

Left Brain

forget majestically, like
miraculous; occurring
mornings, the same as
something together coloured
the knowing
watch you die.
and thin. The
forever in my mouth.
and forgetting.
my sharp
between the spaces
the sea so hard
refused memory.

Hide and Seek

there are flowers
on the mirror
and yes, he knows
the flowers
are not real
but if the flowers
are not real
then maybe
the mirror
is not actually
a mirror
and this old man
he can see
cloudy face
grazed eyes
is his father
and they've just been
playing
at a game
all this time
and now it's over

All the Reasons Why Mollie Can't Go Home

Mollie wants to go home to her mum.
Please, she says, will you help me? I need to get to the bus.
She bullies the lock on every door.
There is something terrible about her feet.
"No. Not now, Mollie - you have your dinner first."
"No. Not just now Mollie - we're waiting for the rain to stop."

Mollie doesn't know how to stop.
She wants to go home to her mum.
And she doesn't have time for a cup of tea first
because she's going to be late for the bus.
"No. Not now Mollie - you're a little unsteady on your feet."
"No. Not just now, Mollie - we haven't the key to that door."

She tells all her secrets to the door.
But sometimes her words seem to stop.
They dirty the floor and her failing feet.
She needs to get home to her mum.
"No. Not now Mollie - this one isn't your bus."
"No. Not just now Mollie - we'll finish this washing up first."

The yellow tablet is swallowed first
from the medicine cart with the flat metal doors.
Sometimes she's inside it and sometimes on the bus.
She's scared but the driver won't stop.
"No, not now Mollie - no I've never met your mum."

"No, not just now Mollie - we need to lift those feet."

They purple, then explode, her feet.
She'll need to see a doctor first.
Can somebody please, telephone her mum?
How long before the pain begins to stop?
"No, not now Mollie - you mustn't go charging at doors."
"No, not just now Mollie - you haven't the money for the bus."

She sees it, through the window, the bus.
But she's wearing someone else's feet.
Something inside her is starting to stop.
She knows that she isn't the first.
"No, not now, Mollie - look, here's your name on this door."
"No, not just now Mollie - you said goodbye to your mum."

She sits down to rest for a little while first.
In a minute, she'll go looking for the door.
There's something she mustn't forget, it's important.
There's something about her mum.

Right Brain

We forget – we all
when we were first
in each other's
how it was he said:
how could I live with
that one day I would
Unbearably glassy;
dirty taste of gone
Of course walls
Of course you always now
flash of light
the lighthouse only loves
because it has

Interview with the Bears

No, of course this isn't what we had in mind at all.
The smells couldn't be more different here
from the clean fruit of a child's head.
They rumple their faces over our beds. Today
we're the wrong kind of children; tomorrow
we're like answers in their hands, bright furry sentences.
It's best not to get too attached.
To ignore the sudden smile in the corridor
or the hug that suggests for once you might be
exactly what they were looking for.
What remain are the stains, the grungy kisses,
the pressure of a teacup around our mouths.
The way they pulled us apart and fingered our innards
endlessly, with joy, like we were snow.

Elizabeth

[

] Silent Mind. [

] Give me Life. [

] Me? [

] He'll get married. [

] School. [

] Frightened. [

] 1, 2, 3, 4, 4, 5, 6, 7 [

] No. [

Angela

Angela: I can do anything I want... I can do anything I want with a needle. But my brothers pick it up and throw it. Two older... Three older... I'm always in the middle. But it doesn't matter. I keep telling them.

I've never been polished at school or anything like that. I used to... I used to draw and Robert used to be a good drawer... Robert's a brother and, yes... If they want me to go anywhere with them and I don't want to go, then I get the fingers poking. It's not fair then. Oh they hurt... Can you see what they do? [*points to her arms and wrists*] It hurts. It hurts all over, and they've always their nails. They do hurt. They say I'm soft. You have no brothers at all?

Sarah: No. And no sisters. Sometimes I wish I had them.

Angela: Sometimes my brothers will come in... They have their own beds and I have my own bed... I lived in a chip shop. Yes, fish and chips - it did smell. Oh awful. But they're not too bad at fending for me. They will say, "Leave her alone!"... things like that. They frighten me... I can beat them. But... it's hard work. That's why I have this little room, with two locks on. So they can't get in.

Yes... yes... my mother had a big family. And her parents had... they had... a lot. More than we had. But I don't bother. I should close that door... close that door. Lock that door. Somebody gave me that, um, bedcoat. That's nice and warm... But I keep thinking I might... look for another school. But I don't know where. And Robert was a good drawer. I couldn't do it, I just couldn't. I was a prefect.

Sarah: Did you learn to sew at school?

Angela: Well, I started to sew when... when I was only tiny I started to sew. And these pieces... all these... I've done all kinds of things... I like these, um... what do you call them?

Sarah: Pleats.

Angela: Yes, I like this kind of work. But they've ripped it off. I've no patience at all with it. And in the night, when it's dark. That door is locked. And... so they can't get in... I don't know what time. You can hear them. You can hear them.

I wish I would have had a couple of sisters. That would have been better. We used to have nuns. Nuns, you know... that's just reminded me because my knee is hurting. That's sore. And I daren't ask them to get me something for it. I'm not soft. Sometimes it's really sore. I'm better off doing something like that... they will sit and watch. They will sit and watch me do that and they will say, "What is that?" and I had to try and think what was what. "Oh, it's an oak tree. That's nothing like an oak tree!"

Catholic school. And they used to... In that blue book... I'm waiting to... that's Preston. Do you know Preston? Have you seen this book? It's a good book is that if you want to read it. It's very good. It tells you all about the teachers and it's really good. Really good... Preston - miniature. You can borrow it. Because I've read it... thousands of times... because if my father sees me reading a book and it isn't perfect he says, "Put that down, it's too old for you." But I, I keep praying, that I will pass my exams so I can go to the college.

Sarah: What do you want to do at college?

Angela: I don't really know. Because no matter what I talk about it's "Oh, you don't do that" and "You don't want to do that." But I do want to do it. I wanted to be a sewer, so, I had it written out. You know, the collars and things... it could do with a really good wash, or dry clean. But they don't... If they see me anywhere... they stop and say, "Where are you going?"... "Well, I'm just going to town."... "The town is no place for you!" So then I don't know what to do. Because I'm frightened of them giving me one.

You don't want any brothers. Oh no, no. Sometimes, in the night, I hear that door. And I'm terrified, because I don't know whether it's them... or whether... what. And my father will call out "Who's playing with that door?" I daren't say anything.

Sarah: Was he a nice man your dad?

Angela: Oh yes, very handsome. Very tall, very tall... and all his own teeth. Yes, he was a very handsome man. And he was in the army. He was in France for a long time... a long long time. Yes. I used to sometimes see his letters... and I'd pick them up... and my father... he would say... there's nothing in that letter for you. Put it down. So I used to put it down again. In his very deep voice... I have some pictures of him. He's a very good looking man. Very black hair... My mum was little and fat. Very little and red hair. She was all right to work for. She would show us what to do. She would show us at the stitchings and then... "Right, everybody, finish now and start! Get your buckets out!"

You know... it used to hurt. All these marks... Mum taught

me how to sew but... you had to do it her way, you couldn't do it your way: "That's not sewing. That's playing around with a needle and cotton." And yet... I could go to the nunnery... and they would teach me. They used to say, "You'll make a marvellous sewer if you just do it." Well, they won't let me. Mother Philippa won't let me.

They were very good... very good at needlework. They were very very good with the needlework. Taking the stitches up... but it used to hurt your eyes. Doing it too long, it used to hurt. You'd say, "Well, it hurts."... "It hurts?! What a needle and thread hurts? That doesn't hurt." But it did hurt... A lady gave me that... jacket, because I was cold one night. And then she said, "What's that for?"... I said, "To keep me warm."... "Why do you want keeping warm? You've a big enough bedroom." I didn't take any notice.

He used to say, "Yes, I've got five boys and I've got one girl." As if he had something, you know? "My girl. One girl. And she can sing and she can act." I couldn't do anything of it, of course! Anything I used to do... oh... not that. So, I used to get to the picture where I didn't even know what my name was.

But I like having friends in, like you coming in... people coming in... Because, when they did... they was on their best behaviour. They wouldn't say anything. And whoever's having their meal they would say, "What did you say your name was? What did you say your name was?" And I'd say, "Angela!"

Sarah: Angela is a very pretty name.

Angela: I think so, but nobody else does. But I had... we had all these things... like... do you ever witness crowning old ladies? We had to make the crown... that was for school. We had to... She would say, "Have you had any sweets today? Or last week?"... "Yes."... "Well, the wire that was in it, would you please take it out and twirl it round until you get a crown?"... Well, sometimes you couldn't see. It used to be hard work. They used to say, "Make a crown out of that piece of..." And I was hopeless. I was hopeless at it. But I used to get through.

I used to go to bed at night... with being the only girl I was the only one in the bedroom and I used to make these things in bed... "I can hear needles! I can hear needles!"... "What kind of needles, mum, can you hear?" I'd say. "I can't hear needles."... "Well, I can hear needles! And if I come in that bedroom someone else will hear needles!"

Sarah: Did you make your own clothes?

Angela: I made a lot of them, yes. Things like this... buttonholes... She'd say, "What's this? A buttonhole? It's nothing of the kind!" A buttonhole is a buttonhole to me... She's hard work, Mother Philippa. She's tall and slim. And she used to walk... like that... and just swish the thing back... swish that one back... and sometimes she hit you in the eye with it... it used to hurt... she was hard work... sometimes she could be different.

We never got paid anything... sometimes you'd get a prize. We didn't get lunch at school. We had to go home for it at school. And she'd say, "Who was clicking the knitting needles! After 12 o'clock!" Well, we'd all been doing it. I didn't know what she was talking about sometimes. Horrible... She had a white... thing round her face... what do you call them?

Sarah: Wimples?

Angela: Wimples... something like that... and then it went round her neck. And my father used to hate it so much. And he used to say, "If you don't take that so and so thing off, I shall come and drag it off!" I used to think, oooh, great! And you could hear her breathing. "I can hear that breathing, can't I Angela Casey!" I didn't know whether to say yes or no because I was frightened.

There would just be big tears coming down. I got home and said to my mother, "She says that your tears should come out of your eyes." But they don't come out of my eyes. She said, "If I ever see tears come out of your eyes I will come and put tears in her eyes!" Terrified. Terrified. I used to skip home. I've gone into... I've gone into... I've gone into the big school... into the big school. And they'd say, "What is the big school? What's the big school? What's the difference between the big school and that school?" I didn't know. But it was better.

Now then, tomorrow, it's the dental day. Oh! The dentist is coming tomorrow. We want to see all your toothbrushes. Bring your toothbrushes. And when he was there he would say, "Can I see your teeth?" It was funny really. And the mother had a... like a black thing on her head... it came around her neck here... and... I didn't know what to do with it.

Sarah: Did you have a school uniform?

Angela: It just depended how you worked... she sometimes...you deserved such a thing. We had a dress... I don't know... sometimes I run away... oh yes... I didn't like it at all, school. I wasn't any good at drawing. I wasn't any good at different things... I didn't like it much... I wasn't any good at singing... "You're not singing! You're just doing the mouth!" They weren't too bad for slapping... Anyway, nearly over, nearly over with, thank goodness.

"Now sing! Sing!" And sometimes I didn't even know the words they wanted. This black thing across here... it was a cap... and down here... and down her neck... it nearly touched the floor... this was a wimple and this was a... I didn't know what they were called... and I used to go home and say to my mother, "We had to wear a wimple today." And I remember my mother saying, "What's a wimple?" She didn't know what a wimple was and neither did I.

Anyway, I got through. I got through it. And if you got through you got a chest like that. Yes, we got that. It's nice. Now all the sewing things that I've made are in there [*gestures at wardrobe*] if you want to look at them... behind that door was the stairs... and you used to fly down the stairs because you were so fed up of what was going on. But many a time we all fell down... we all fell down.

The teacher... I could never understand what she was talking about. I said to my dad one day, "I'm going to set fire to that school." And he said "Why?" And I said, "Because I don't know what she's talking about." But then we had to take it all out. Everything had to be washed and polished and shut again. It used to drive me crazy. But the door... and that door... and this, had to be pure white. Otherwise... trouble. It was frightening. I didn't like it. So I hope you never get there.

Anyway... it's very warm in here.

Sarah: Would you like to go for a walk in the garden?

Angela: I would have to ask. If she said I could move, she would say yes. But she was always in these long robes, right to the floor. Black. Used to be murder. And the boys used to come in and start laughing... I brought some material. She said, "What's that for?" I said, "Because I like it."... "Well, you can just put it away because you're not going to use it." So you didn't get much... you didn't get much happiness from what you did... I used to ask my mother, what I could do. She used to say, "It's there for you to see."

And they never used to talk about what would you do if, if you were getting married. Well, you didn't know what you were doing even if you were getting married. So I said, at the table, one day to my mother, "What do you do when you get married?" She said, "What do you mean?" I said, "It's the lesson for the tomorrow." And she said, "Well, tell the teacher to mind her own business!" So I went on and asked my mother and she said, "Nosey parkers will be something else." I could never understand it... If you could read the Latin in so many weeks you'd done very well. Of course it isn't easy... and I used to hate it and didn't say anything.

We never used to learn any poetry or anything. It was all... "What colour is that wall?" No, I didn't like it much. We didn't get a lot of poetry. If you open those doors, in that drawer, you'll see a lot of writing... a lot of writing... and if you read it... it was like poetry.

They had to be right. The white had to be the white and the red had to be the red. And I used to hate it. The boys didn't get that though. They boys were opposite. In the same street but opposite. I didn't like it. I was all boys at home. I didn't want it at night. My mother would say, "Have you been crying?"... "No."... "You have."... "Well, she said that I should know by now, that I should know it and I don't know it."..."Write it down and we'll learn it." And we'd go all night, learning. But I didn't know it in the morning.

And then of course you're the teacher's pet. So I'm hoping that I pass... something like that... if I could pass with that.

Mother Philippa. Yes, who was the other one? The other one was a little fat nun. Very round face. Mother Philippa was a tall, slim lady. And she used to always sling her... behind her. I had to have a confirmation. And we used to have a crown... and a white dress. Auntie Lizzie made my dress. Auntie Lizzie was a good sewer. Better than me, and she used to teach me. Really, when you think, it wasn't too bad. You didn't get slapped. You never got slapped. But they were... Yes... my Auntie Lizzie bought me that material for a birthday. It is nice really. I could just pop it in warm water and it used to come out beautiful. I used to think... what on earth will we do with that, but it got all right. It got all right. I think the nuns lived in a different world than we did. They didn't want to know what we did. We didn't want to know what they did. She could look over your shoulder at what you were doing... right down. I didn't like that. My father didn't do anything like that. He would push you but he wouldn't hit you. I don't know what I'm going to do next. I don't know yet. I would like to write... I don't know... what do you write about when you've nothing to write about? If you've nothing...

Sarah: You've got a whole life to write about.

Angela: Yes, but they say that's rubbish. It wasn't... we got through. It was quite... You see I had five brothers. That mirror, on my wall... now one of my brothers made that. He said, "I've got something for you." And he put it there. I was thrilled to bits. But it wasn't there long... before it was smashed.

Which school do you go to? One teacher used to say,

"Attention!" So you had to stand up. I don't know. I just seemed to dislike it from the beginning to the end. I wouldn't co-operate with any of it. I wouldn't try. Because I thought well, if it's wrong, I'll be in trouble. Oh no. As long as we get through it and go somewhere else... but I never seem to get anywhere else. My lips are always sore and I never know why they're sore. Anyway, not to worry. I'm going to wash that one day. And if it doesn't wash right... I'll have to try. It is hurting. My mother taught me how to machine. And my aunt taught me how to machine. But they were frightened of me breaking it. It's all right. It isn't so many more years to go and then I'll fly out of that room, I will. When the boys come and poke... I'm not going to worry about it anymore. A while back, it was just a nice day. I looked out of the window and I thought... I'll go, I'll run home. But when I got to the turn... at the road... she was stood there. She said, "Where are you going? What are you doing?"... "Oh, mother, I'm lost."

I don't know what I'm going to do next. I don't know what I'd like to do. I want to do all this kind of work. But that will have to be washed. I will ask my mother anyway. She's a better washer. But one day... I will run away. Definitely... I shall run away... because I can't stand it. I don't know what I'll do, but I will run away. Because I don't like it. Like this school that I'm in now. You're never right. You're never right. So on a nice day... something like this... a few weeks ago... I said to one of them, "Shall we run away?" And she said, "What do you mean? Shall we run away?" I said, "Shall we run away? Away from all this?" Anyway, it's not too bad... Do you... do you not go anywhere else but in this school?

Sarah: Yes, I go home.

The Hard Words

Look, let's be clear: don't imagine
there is anybody here who enjoys
dribbling poetry. If you think we're
holding stars on our tongues
that's your eyes want testing.
If you hear music when we grunt
you haven't understood exactly
what it is we needed to say.
You might enjoy the ruins
of our grammar, the way we
chew up our nouns to song.
It's not your hand that's getting
thinner on the blanket.
Please don't ask us to speak
the hard words all at once.

Communion

What's this? A coincidence
of pale bread in the mouth.

Oh, it couples with her tongue like snow.

And someone is talking of lovely things;

of a man whose heart is an unknown city,
of how her bones will be shot through with silver.

Is she expected somewhere this evening?
Will she be required to dance?

Shall thy wonders be known in the dark?
And thy righteousness in the land of forgetfulness?

Jack

Jack was married in 1955. *it's been a violent week, one way or another, disagreements and what have you* Jack did National Service in the Royal Army Medical Corps. *you find out when the sun shines who your friends are, and we haven't so many* Jack worked as a paint stripper at BAE systems in Preston. *we had fun, intelligent fun* Jack has no problems with hearing at this time.

Jack can hold a reasonable conversation though will sometimes drift between past and present. *there you are, best fold it over, wrap it in World War 2* Jack has a very good sense of humour. *here I am, waiting for an ordinary... that's as far as I can get*

Jack loves to talk about fishing. *I fell in, long before these ever came* Jack would probably enjoy reading/looking at books about fishing. Jack is unable to do any fishing due to his arthritic hands. Jack has a fluctuating memory. *no, I'm lost* Jack's speech is quite clear, but he requires time to process information and respond. *at least you can find him when you want him* Jack is disorientated to time and place.

Jack will sometimes use a knife and fork but when unable to manage he likes to use a spoon. *Here's Paddy! I'll give him two hammers!* Jack's family have requested that Jack is enabled to have a biscuit with his afternoon tea. *The Bishop will want a go for himself.* Jack requires staff to enable a fresh change of clothes on a daily basis.   *well, certain little things have happened*

Jack should be enabled the reasonable right to risk.   *I had the job of swinging the thurible, not all the way round, just side to side* Jack has little insight into his own safety and risk.   *it spilt on the steps, it nearly set the green steps on fire!   but there's plenty of water in a Catholic Church!*   Jack should be enabled to see visiting entertainers.   Jack enjoys entertainment.

Jack had a triple bypass sixteen years ago. Following this operation a small piece of metal   *one particular night... no, I've forgotten*   was left protruding from his chest.

Jack may have sad moments (family advised).

Jack prefers the bedroom door closed and the light turned off. *you get used to it or you don't get used to it*   Jack wears pyjamas. *there's one, jumping with a parachute*

you don't know whether to stop or whether to go slow, do you? you're going to run out of paper

This Place

When my time comes
and I ask you
again and again where I am
you'll be able to tell me, truthfully
that this place is a train
that I know quite well

    Calling at:
Warrington Bank Quay
Wigan Northwestern
Preston

    Calling at:
Wigan Northwestern
Warrington Bank Quay
and London Euston, where this journey terminates

    Calling at:

CPSIA information can be obtained
at www.ICGtesting.com
Printed in the USA
BVOW08s1439260318
511604BV00004B/643/P

9 781908 058225